STEPHANIE LIMB
My Coleridge

BROKEN SLEEP BOOKS

All rights reserved; no part of this book
may be reproduced by any means
without the publisher's permission.

Published 2020,
Broken Sleep Books:
Talgarreg, Wales

brokensleepbooks.com

The author has asserted their right to be
identified as the author of this Work in
accordance with the Copyright, Designs
and Patents Act 1988

Lay out your unrest.

Publisher/Editor: Aaron Kent

Typeset in UK by Aaron Kent

Broken Sleep Books is committed to
a sustainable future for our planet,
and therefore uses print on
demand publication.

brokensleepbooks@gmail.com

ISBN: 9798608584053

For Sara

My Coleridge:
On six poems by Sara Coleridge

Stephanie Limb

'Passion is blind not love: her wondrous might'

Passion is blind not Love: her wondrous might
Informs with three-fold pow'r man's inward sight: –
To her deep glance the soul at large displayed
Shews all its mingled mass of light and shade: –
Men call her blind when she but turns her head,
Nor scans the fault for which her tears are shed.
Can dull indifference or Hate's troubled gaze
See through the secret heart's mysterious maze? –

Can Scorn and Envy pierce that 'dread abode',
Where true faults rest beneath the eye of God?
Not theirs, 'mid inward darkness, to discern
The spiritual splendours how they shine and burn.
All bright endowments of a noble mind
They, who with joy behold them, soonest find;
And better none its stains of frailty know
Than they who fain would see them white as snow.[1]

On inward sight

Sometimes my son purses his lips and moves them onto the side of his face. I'm startled. My face remembers what that expression feels like. I know it's mine. Ours.

Recognition drew me to Sara Coleridge. I glanced at her – a deep glance – saw something familiar. That's what I look for, in words, something familiar. When I'm looking at someone

I love, or recognise, I don't want to see the shameful parts. I can't stop myself from looking. I notice more. I look furtively – with a burn of shame. Feeling perverse. A deep glance breaches boundaries. It feels indecent.

Looking though her father's notebooks – Sara saw herself. Looking at her brother – she saw herself. After Hartley's death she wrote:

> But some have suggested that we do not perhaps know the extent of his excesses. Alas! who *should* know them better – or half as well as – myself, who all of my life long in one shape or another have been a sufferer by them.[2]

Looking at Sara – I see myself.

Inward sight is partial. Views are always partial. Sara understood this. In her introduction to *Biographia Literaria* she wrote, 'I for my part, have not striven to conceal my partialities, or to separate my love for my father from my moral and intellectual sympathy for his mode of thought.'[3] The inward sight that Sara describes doesn't split love from thought. It captures the wet-brown organs and clean-white bone in the snap of one glance.

Sara wrote 'Passion is blind not love' in response to her father's fragment:

> I have heard of reasons manifold
> Why Love must needs be blind,
> But this the best of all I hold –
> His eyes are in his mind.

> What outward form and feature are
> He guesseth but in part;
> But that within is good and fair
> He seeth with the heart.

Samuel Taylor Coleridge (STC) describes objective sight coming from the mind and love's sight from the heart – seeing within. Sara's concept of love's sight is more like Roland Barthes' *punctum*, 'A photograph's *punctum* is that accident which pricks me (but also bruises me, is poignant to me).'[4] Love sees more. More deeply. More light. More shade. Everything bared – by the viewed and the viewer – in one X-ray flash: the crusted liver, the opium-slowed guts bulging like a sock full of rocks. Sara was the person best equipped to edit her father because she loved him. More than love – she saw herself. When writing about him, she exposed herself.

Virginia Woolf wrote about Sara:

> The whole of her forty-eight years were lived in the light of his sunset, so that, like other children of great men, she is a chequered dappled figure flitting between a vanished radiance and the light of every day. And, like so many of her father's works, Sara Coleridge remains unfinished […] That extremely interesting fragment, her autobiography, ends with three rows of dots after twenty-six pages.[5]

Woolf's sight was also partial and obscured – she had no access to most of Sara's poetry, essays and letters. Sara began a memoir when she was dying of cancer – written as a letter to her daughter, Edith. She abandoned it to work on another edition of STC's poems. I know how it looks [. . .] but Sara didn't leave any dots. Leaving dots wasn't her style. Even Sara's colons are often followed by dashes. A pause: a line – joining thoughts. Sara was more likely to draw lines and make connections: – a dot to dot.

'On reviewing my early childhood, I find the predominant reflection'

She stops. No dots. Not one. Not even a full stop.

Sara once wrote:

> Sometimes I have had thoughts of an autobiography. I believe the life of any individual, related sincerely and accurately in its more characteristic features – an abstract giving the quintessence of the individual experience, would be interesting and valuable. But then the difficulty would be to avoid exposing others.[6]

Sara struggled to extract the 'quintessence' of her childhood. She piled on words – like stones on a torturer's press – to squeeze out quintessence. As the past presses towards the present it becomes impossible to write sincerely and accurately without exposing others.

How to write to Edith about becoming a mother?

> Quintessence, (n): In classical and medieval philosophy: a fifth essence existing in addition to the four elements, supposed to be the substance of which the celestial bodies were composed and to be latent in all things; (*Alchemy*) this essence, supposed to be able to be extracted by distillation or other procedures.[7]

I imagine Sara pouring the 'diary of her children's early years' into a pot still. Sara, scraping those black words from the page – like insects, crisped and pressed – rattling off the paper into the still. She pours in sugar – stuffs herbs in the neck. The vapours condense. A bitter liquid collects. It retains a familiar red-brown tincture. Fumes to make your eyes water. Is that her quintessence? – one sniff could knock you out.

Laudanum, (n): The simple alcoholic tincture of opium.[8]

It feels seedy rooting though Sara's diary – like I'm poking around in her pants drawer. Or her pants – she logs every vaginal discharge in her diary. Cyprine is a French word for vaginal lubrication. Lisa Robertson writes, 'Maybe Cyprine, or syntax is the fifth element.'[9] The fifth element – quintessence. Is quintessence extracted from between the legs? Does it look like egg whites – albumen? Spooling and binding.

Sara found her father – after he died, in his notebooks. She also inherited a literary house that was crumbling. She pieced it together. She used her quintessence as glue (or mortar) to make STC cohere. She drew lines and joined dots. She built. It's impossible to write about Sara without writing about her father – not because she's a continuation of him – because he is a continuation of her. 'Throughout, Sara appealed to STC as one of his disciples, but she also manipulated his ideas and writings for her own ends.'[10]

Sara enjoyed scholarly work – 'I do not want *thanks* for my little labours – because I like these literary examinations for their own ends' – but it obscured her. Sometimes obscurity feels safe. Other times it's frustrating – 'No work is so inadequately rewarded either by money or credit as that of editing miscellaneous, fragmentary, immethodical lit remains like those of STC.'[11]

Editing is creative. Posthumous editing is invention. Sara authored her father. Sara (the author) stood behind Sara (the editor) – her essays scuttled behind STC and hid. Editing was a screen but the thanklessness was an insult. Writing in disgust to her brother: 'I am opposed under the name of *Mr.* Nelson Coleridge—Mr. C's *son*—my words of *course* misrepresented.'[12]

When Sara met Elizabeth Barrett-Browning she wrote:

> She would have so much to gratify her and make her happy (spite of the paternal unreconcileableness) but for weak health. But that is such a want! She takes morphine three times a day.[13]

The stains of frailty we notice in other people reveal our stains of frailty. Some of Sara's frailties stand out to me – make me squirm. Reading her diary, I experience *punctum*. It feels like seeing a smear of my menstrual blood on the seat pad in a fancy restaurant. I'm exposed. This is more than recognition.

Inward sight is like a camera obscura – allowing us to see the brightest light. I need to stand inside the dark to see the brightness of Sara's candour. Sara became more candid – reaching a triumphant crescendo in her passionate, defiantly partial defences of STC in 1847. It would be shoddy to admire her candour without reciprocating. I want to meet her halfway. Or some of the way.

A note on gloss –

Sara's editor, Pete Swaab writes, 'Many of her footnotes digress and expand into short essays, always cogent in themselves but of dubious relevance to the text that they gloss, excursions from it and not elucidations.'[14] I like the idea of glossing a text. I think of those shiny signs at old-fashioned fairgrounds. Festoon lights around glossily-illuminated manuscripts.

My experiences are gloss in the margins, but – like STC's 1817 gloss on 'The Ancient Mariner' – maybe they bully the reader. My gloss, like Sara's footnotes, excurses rather than elucidates. My gloss is glossolalia – the incoherent language and mangled syntax of the hysteric.

Or my gloss is quintessence – discharge. Albumen – holding the double yolk of me and Sara. This quintessence-gloss – shellacked over Sara's poems – has hardened into a lens helping me to see more light. More shade. Or a thin, pretty doppelganger – a character I've invented to refract my experience of motherhood one hundred and eighty years into the past.

Verses written in sickness 1833, before the Birth of Berkeley and Florence

My babe unborn, I dream of thee,
   Foreshaping all thy looks and wiles,
But Heaven's light may close on me,
Ere I thy real face can see
   Ere I can watch thy dawning smiles.

My older children round my heart
   For many a day have been entwined:
Yet dear to me, e'en now, thou art;
Fain would I do a Mother's part
   Ere life and love are both resigned.

You will not droop, my precious dears,
   When I am numbered with the dead:
You ne'er can know my cares and fears;
Your eyes will fill with childish tears,
   Which o'er my grave will not be shed.

When others weep and mourn for me
   That I no longer must be here,
Ne'er may they quench your childish glee;
No sadness ever may you see
   To check the laugh of thoughtless cheer.

But when you gain reflection's dow'r
   O ne'er thus joyless may you pine!
Ne'er may you know the anguished hour,

The sickening fears that overpower
   This crushed but struggling heart of mine.

In dreams an airy course I take
   And seem my tedious couch to fly:
Or o'er the bosom of the lake
Ere to captivity I wake,
   My skimming boat I swiftly ply.

But nought my waking hours can bless –
   I strive to sweeten Sorrow's cup;
'Tis all in vain, for ne'ertheless
I find it dregged with bitterness,
   When to my lips I lift it up.

My griefs are not to be expressed:
   Affection's voice can charm no more:
I ne'er shall find a steady rest,
Till torn from all I love the best,
   I seek the distant unknown shore.[15]

On sorrow's cup

In 1833 the maternal mortality rate was around 5%. Women often bought winding sheets along with their lying-in clothes. This makes me think of Co-op Funeralcare next door to Mamas and Papas; putting down a deposit on an expensive pushchair – and a coffin.

Although Sara could expect better medical treatment than many, she'd had complications when delivering Edith in 1832. She was dangerously ill with puerperal fever. Multiple gestations increase the risks for the mother – the risk of eclampsia, haemorrhage, thrombosis and infection multiply with every baby a woman pushes out. She had every reason to be terrified. This poem is staged from the perspective of an expectant mother – these fears don't feel entirely based on the physical stakes, although the physical stakes were high: Berkerley and Florence were born in January 1834 and survived only a few days.

Edith was born in July 1832. She was a difficult baby. Sara's diary entries repeatedly refer to Edith's wind, 'Darling E. 2 months old. She had some little windy motions today with some pain. She still suffers from wind but sleeps well. Her bowels have not been quite regular since my being poorly.'[16] Sara blamed herself for Edith's 'wind.' Wind is code for 'colic' – a term uncoined in the 19th Century. Colic strikes at week three, which coincides with Sara's puerperal fever (there was no need to blame herself – although I understand – mothers generally blame themselves).

My first baby has colic. I am convinced it is my fault. My milk – it comes too fast and Ted has to gulp – he is bloated by the time the hindmilk comes through. I buy an electric breast pump and express before I feed. The pump makes a groaning sound that worms into my ear. Constantly, I hear a baby crying or the groan of breast pump.

Pump. Feed. Rock. Repeat.

I hold Ted, massage his stomach, lay with him against my chest, rhythmically rub his white-cottoned back. Try to rub the air from his guts. I hope every bubble and pop will soothe him. Shut him up. I force Infacol into his mouth with a sticky pipette. He spits it into a noose – gummed in the folds of his neck – gathering fluff, vomit and milk.

As soon as he falls asleep my body is humming. My brain counts the hours – the minutes – I have before he will wake. Adrenaline and cortisol pinball synapses. I grind my head into the pillow – trying to penetrate the surface of sleep. The sound of the breast pump keeps groaning in my head. I'll swallow anything to help me sleep: valerian; nutmeg shavings in warm milk; antihistamines – sometimes, wine.

I go to the doctor for something stronger. I give up pumping and buy formula – my milk is polluted with drugs. Mastitis grows in lumps on my breasts – boils on my areola. I am swollen – engorged from all that pumping. I go back to the doctor. I peel back my bra – he prods my deformed tits. Prescribes.

Everything leaks. My breasts. My vagina. My eyes.

'Fain would I do a Mother's part' – Sara often uses the word 'fain' to mean 'gladly' but it also meant 'obliged.' With 'fain' coming so close to 'resigned' her meaning feels more aligned with obligation. Resignation – 'Alas! Alas!' For ten year's Sara's diary is full of 'alas'. Sara's ambivalence to motherhood had sharpened by 1833. Giving birth to Edith swallowed her. She barely slept. She began to use opiates. The worry about the use of opiates kept her awake. She swallowed more opiates. She wept most days. She often uses the word 'hysterical.' Hysteria – from the Greek word for womb. During the nineteenth century the link between reproduction and hysteria meant Britain was experiencing an epidemic of 'puerperal madness.' The date of Sara's first illness slices through the epi-curve – almost central – the graph flayed like a torn perineum. Sara wrote to Elizabeth Wardell in March 1833, 'This dreadful hysterical depression poisons everything. Alas! I seem to be mother and no mother.'[17]

Sara had few options available to her except marriage and motherhood – few options, none of them her first choice. Before she married, Sara wrote to her brother – Derwent, 'The thing that would suit me the best of anything in the world would be the life of a country Clergyman. I should delight in the studies necessary to that profession.'[18]

Sara grew up with Robert Southey. She spent much of her childhood at Wordsworth's cottage. She wrote, 'To my Uncle Southey I owe much—to his books—to his example—his life, and conversation—far more. But to Mr. W. and my father I owe my *thoughts* more than to all other men put together.'[19] Wordsworth's 'Ode to Immortality' addresses the mighty prophet – the innocent child: 'Heaven lies about us in our infancy!' Every step away from birth takes us further from the 'visionary gleam' of paradise. But Sara's attitude to the innocence of childhood isn't Wordsworth's – she doesn't owe these thoughts to her fathers. Sara's poem begins like a benevolent blessing – a dying fairy [god]mother addressing her unborn child – 'Ne'er may they quench your childish glee.' Then the glee of the child begins to feel like spite, 'No sadness ever may you see/ To check the laugh of thoughtless cheer.'

The innocent child is not Wordsworth's mighty prophet.

The innocent child is 'thoughtless'.

The child is not innocent at all.

The child is – simply – ignorant.

Jonathan Bate reviewed Sara Coleridge's *Collected Poems* (2007) in *The Guardian* on Saturday 10th March, 2007. His verdict:

The critic Harold Bloom famously read the Romantic poets in terms of "the anxiety of influence", arguing that their creativity stemmed from an Oedipal reaction against their canonical predecessors. "Strong" poets are those who throw off the burden of the father and find a voice that is fully their own. Sara had courage and technical ability, but not the strength to take poetic language to places undiscovered by her father and his circle.

What a male lens to view a 'strong' poet. Gilbert and Gubar write,

> the "anxiety of influence" that a male poet experiences is felt by the female poet as an even more primary "anxiety of authorship"— a radical fear that she cannot create, that because she can never become a "precursor" the act of writing will isolate or destroy her.[20]

Sara could not take her father's place – as a female. But Sara didn't merely imitate. She sneaked into her father's texts and published her own ideas – by stealth. By acting as a daughter, she took over the body of her father['s work]. She threw off the 'burden of her father' by manipulating his image into a reflection of hers. Sara had the strength to contradict Wordsworth's concept of childhood innocence, in this, and other poems. Sara wrote about a domestic world 'undiscovered by her father' – STC left his family in the care of Robert Southey before she was born. She had the strength to write honestly about the ambivalence of motherhood in a language sweetened with sentimentality but with dregs of irony – at the bottom of the cup – spat from her tongue.

Sara looked for other female precursors. Her letters reveal how closely she read: Harriet Martineau, Joanna Baillie, Felicia Hemans, Anna Laetitia Barbauld and Elizabeth Barrett Browning, but Sara was a tricky customer. A journal entry in April 1835 reads, 'few women are profound.' Then goes on, 'many have clearer perceptions, keener observations, a nicer tact – a more original fancy – a more imaginative turn, more earnest reflectiveness – a more stabilising intellect'[21] Jeez, who needs to be profound? I'd take all that! – but Sara couldn't find the female poet she needed. The female poet-precursor who would allow her to publish poetry. She was gagged by her own narrow definition of a 'strong poet.' Her ambivalence to the female poet meant she only published poetry 'fit for four-year olds' – unable to call her own poetry profound. What did she mean by profound? Insight? Quintessence?

Sara stops short of wishing this baby will experience her 'sickening fears', but by addressing these fears to the unborn child she spells out what this new life cost her. She stops short of wishing her sorrows on the child. Just. Yet, she makes it clear – birthing children was killing her.

Opiates have a bitter taste. Laudanum was often sweetened with brandy and spices but it was still bitter. By 1833 Sara was struggling to sweeten motherhood with opiates. In this poem she sweetens motherhood with sentimentality but it remains 'dregged with bitterness.' The dregs become a verb that infuse the whole drink – the bitter overpowering the sweet.

Laudanum is not my drug. The NHS don't prescribe it. I can't buy it in the local pharmacy – I am given zopiclone to help me sleep. It also tastes bitter. The metallic aftertaste is a hangover in my mouth. I sugar my tongue but the metal cuts through. I'd have become dependent on laudanum if I'd given birth in 1832. I don't believe in 'addictive personalities' and I don't believe Sara inherited her addiction. Anyone can become an addict. It is circumstance.

Poppies

The Poppies blooming all around
  My Herbert loves to see;
Some pearly white, some dark as night,
  Some red as cramasie:

He loves their colours fresh and fine
  As fair as fair may be;
But little does my darling know
  How good they are to me.

He views their clust'ring petals gay,
  And shakes their nut-brown seeds;
But they to him are nothing more
  Than other brilliant weeds.

O! how shouldst thou, with beaming brow,
  With eye and cheek so bright,
Know aught of that gay blossom's power,
  Or sorrows of the night?

When poor Mama long restless lies,
  She drinks the poppy's juice;
That liquor soon can close her eyes,
  And slumber soft produce:

O then my sweet, my happy boy
  Will thank the Poppy-flower,

Which brings the sleep to dear Mama,
At midnight's darksome hour.[22]

'In regard to the use of stimulants and narcotics'

Sara Coleridge, 'On Nervousness.'

When the Health Visitor calls in, she says, 'How is mum feeling today? Are mum's stitches healing?' It is disorientating to hear yourself addressed in the third person. As though the Health Visitor is asking the baby these questions and you are answering on his behalf. I wonder if I should sit the baby on my lap like a ventriloquist's dummy and answer:

'Mum feels woozy from lack of sleep. Mum's skin smells of cheese. Mum still holds toilet paper against her vagina every time she goes for a shit because she's scared her insides will fall out. Mum feels as though her quintessence is leaking from every orifice.'

'Oh dear. Could mum fill in the "Edinburgh Postnatal Depression Scale?"'

It is generally believed that Sara would have been diagnosed with post-partum depression after the birth of Edith. I looked at Sara's diary eight weeks after Edith's birth and filled in the 'Edinburgh Postnatal Depression Scale' on her behalf. She scores 27/30 by my reckoning.

I'm not such a neat fit.

In the first few weeks of Ted's life I have an anxiety that is only relieved by nursing him. When he sucks my milk I feel calm – as though he as sucking all the tension away. This is chemical. I understand. A woman breastfeeds – her brain releases oxytocin. I overfeed him for this chemical fix. His measurements skip over the 98th percentile – off the chart of his red book – but I can't produce enough milk to take the anxiety away. It begins to overwhelm me. This is not unexpected. I've been waiting – watching for it. Like Sara, I've always struggled with nervousness.[23]

This is a return of my old nervousness – no different to previous spells – only amplified by a new set of neuroses. Pink, wrinkled nervousness – swaddled in a white cotton package – cries going off like an alarm unless I plug him onto a nipple. Another reason to keep feeding. Maternity leave gives me nothing to think about – apart from the baby. My brain likes to chew – it snags and repeats when it's not got nothing to play. I worry about anything I can think up. I analyse every remark on my mothering. I find it difficult to understand how I am responsible for this human. I know what has happened but can't understand why I didn't evolve into a mother. Or revolve. Motherhood is revolution not evolution. Shouldn't I have changed in some essential way? But mostly, I worry about sleep. I worry that I am selfish for caring about nothing but my own sleep? Why can't I sleep when I am so tired?

At the end of *Motherhood* by Sheila Heti, the protagonist's antidepressants start to kick in – she's amazed. She says she can't believe those pills are legal. I remember the first night I took a sleeping pill. It felt like alchemy. A tincture of magic. There's a poem by STC, one that only survives because Sara noted it down in the margins of her collected works of STC:

> Come damn it, Girls, don't let's be sad,
> The bottle stands so handy;
> Drink gin, if brandy can't be had,
> > But if it can, drink brandy.
> And if old aunts, oh d— their chops,
> > In scolding vent their phthisick,
> Drop in of laudanum thirty drops,
> And call it opening physic. –
> For it opens the heart and it opens the brain,
> And if you once take it, you'll take it again,
> Oh! Jacky, Jacky, Jacky Dandy,
> Laudanum's a great improver of Brandy.[24]

Come damn it – zopiclone is handy. Reliable sleep – if only for four hours. I take a pill and twenty minutes later the room looks furry. Muscles loosen. It's 'opening physic' – everything feels possible. I am a merry drunk. All will be well – until I wake – four or five hours later. Heart banging. Head buzzing – like maggots have eaten my brain and thoughts are flies that zip around my head. My doctor writes an open prescription – warns me to be frugal … but 'if you once take it, you'll take it again.' There are other pills but their effects are more gradual.

My husband wants another baby. My parents want another grandchild. My mother-in-law asks me when I'll *have another*. Strangers ask me when I'll *have another*. Everyone tells me how weird and spoiled *only* children are. In September 1832 Sara begged her husband for 'a three years respite from child-bearing.'[25] I am lucky – I have three years respite.

Ted is three when he asks for a brother or sister. I feel hot, sticky with shame. I decide to do something. I research my medication. I see experts in perinatal psychiatry. I find a combination and dose where the risks don't seem to overshadow the benefits. There are still risks – in the shadows. I cross titrate. I can't sleep for thinking about the risks, which makes it tricky to give up the sleeping pills.

I can't make up my mind about this second baby. I expect another child to throw me back into the worst days of my nervousness, but part of me wants to get it done with – stop the nagging. Finally, I want to stop thinking. Tired of reading observational studies on different SSRI antidepressants – I come off the contraceptive pill. We use condoms. We stop buying condoms.

When Ted runs down steep hills he closes his eyes so that he 'isn't scared'. I explain to him that this doesn't diminish the risks (increases the risks), but what he can't see – can't scare. I shut my eyes. One morning, I tell my husband not to pull out – I feel reckless. Brave – even? Fate! – bring it on. Three weeks later my breasts feel like bruises. I know. I still do a test. I cry. I'm not brave. How could I think I'd be able to do this? I see my doctor – she says, 'pull it together or terminate.' But there isn't really a choice, is there?

On 1st October, 1833 Sara writes, 'Dread of miscarriage. Took 60 drops of morphine.'[26] Sara shut her eyes. I understand – all I want is bed – a couple of pills and a glass of brandy. It's possible that Sara understood there was a link between the miscarriages and morphine but she didn't have any data. I have data. Bold print in leaflets warning off use during pregnancy. I can't plead ignorance.

Sara and I aren't the first and last to medicate motherhood. The image of Valium popping mothers of the sixties is iconic but very few people write about taking prescription drugs when the baby is in utero.

The subject is taboo – even though thousands of women are prescribed psychotropic drugs during pregnancy, Sara and I still feel like we're doing something illicit.

'Poppies' was originally published in a book called *Pretty Lessons in Verse for Good Children* (1834). In the copy she sent to Dora Wordsworth there is a handwritten annotation in the margin:

> Some other of my Herby Cards should have been put in for these rhymes – but there were mistakes in the arrangement of the small vol. at the press – lines crossed out left in v.v . These however were retained through inattention on my part.[27]

Sara also wrote to Emily Trevenen:

> Will you tell Mary that the Poppy poem in "Pretty Lessons" should have been left out – some other doggerel substituted, but I was poorly and Henry in a hurry when the small vol. was arranged.[28]

Her family tried to persuade Sara to remove 'Poppies' from *Pretty Lessons* – there was enough gossip about Coleridgean opium-sots. Despite these notes to friends the collection went through five editions and 'Poppies' remained. Sara claimed inattention for her rebellion. It was rebellion.

'In short the printing of Benoni – and that title – were a fancy of Henry's.'[29] Sara's husband named this book and pushed it out to publication – as though it was his child. Sara nicknamed *Pretty Lessons,* Benoni – the son of Rachel and Jacob (named by his dying mother) – meaning 'son of sorrow.'

I named my second son Sid. I sometimes joke that it's short for Accident.

Pretty Lessons was Sara's first publication after her marriage, she was always half ashamed of it, but it paid the doctor's bills. After Edith, Sara's books were the only babies to survive. She had several miscarriages – the twins died, another daughter died (after only a few days) – Sara would write, 'that frail little baby, partook so largely of her mother's bodily weakness.'[30] blaming herself and, perhaps, the opium she'd been prescribed.

There is a gap between the child's innocence and the mother's experience in 'Poppies'. Herbert isn't a 'Seer blest!'[31] He doesn't appreciate the poppies. I can see Herbert pulling up flowers; snapping off seed heads; popping insects – like pustules – under his fingers. There's an American colloquialism for Oxycontin – 'A Redneck's Rattle'. When a toddler rattles a bottle of opioids, it's noise – giving the world texture. Herbert shakes those 'nut brown seeds' but he can't read the label. There is no label – no meaning. The child experiences the poppy with his senses. He sees the colours, hears the sounds, feels the texture – but his experience is empty of meaning – senseless. In 'Poppies' the adult experience is richer than the child's because the senses and the mind inform the experience.

There are other Romantic opium poems. Henrietta O'Neill's poem 'Ode to the Poppy,' published by Charlotte Smith in 1794 addresses the Poppy, 'I hail the Goddess for her scarlet flower!/ Thou brilliant weed.'[32] Sara calls up O'Neill's poem.

> Mr Dequincey is again on sociable terms with the Wordsworths – he is well in tolerable spirits & has left off

the opium, but Miss W. now fears he will take to the horrid drug again – *horrid* I call it when thinking of him and others, in me that is rather ungrateful, as it has done me much good & no harm and I might exclaim with Miss O Neil "Hail lovely blossom that cans't ease , the wretched victim of disease."[33]

Sara's first taste of laudanum was five years before she had children. Laudanum was part of every medicine cabinet. It did everything: it was paracetamol, it was Lemsip, it was Benylin, it was Feminax, it was Valium, it was Prozac, it was Imodium. When Sara began her habitual use of laudanum, it was originally prescribed for diarrhoea:

> For the last weak I have had a slight bowel complaint, in a good deal of pain with a slight tendency to diarrhoea […] I took twice 10 drops of laudanum prescribed by Henry.[34]

Laudanum was miraculous. I can't imagine a twenty-first century poem apostrophising any drug – without a tincture of shame. We're squeamish about chemical solutions. We have a better understanding of addiction. In 1834 overindulgence in opium was decadence – *moral insanity* – a weak will.

De Quincey, the famous 'Opium Eater' was Sara's first crush! She wrote in her memoirs, 'I remember how Mr. De Quincey jested with me on the journey, and declared I was to be his wife, which I partly believed. I thought he behaved faithlessly in not claiming my hand.'[35] I can't help thinking he would have been a better choice than Henry. De Quincey and Sara were equally matched intellectually – and Sara liked men who idolised her father.

From September 1832, Sara rarely (if ever) slept without opium. Despite the apparent shamelessness in 'Poppies,' she struggled to justify her use. In her essay 'Nervousness' she writes:

> Invalid. Another cause of conscience with me is in regard to the use of stimulants and narcotics, particularly laudanum. Every medical man speaks ill of the drug, prohibits it, & after trying in vain to give me sleep without it, ends with prescribing it himself.
>
> Good Genius. In these cases we must try to make out whether the suffering or the remedy be the greater evil, being honest with ourselves in the inquiry […] we must never think of taking it to procure positive comfort, but only to ward off obstinate sleeplessness, and that not so much on account of the immediate suffering as the after injurious effects of irritation and fatigue.[36]

I've discussed addiction with many people: psychiatrists, therapists, friends. I've read a lot. I'm no expert. I've found some who would agree with Sara that there is a line between 'taking it to procure positive comfort' and 'to ward off obstinate …' To me, this sounds like the logic of an addict. Isn't warding off a horrible symptom also procuring comfort? Maybe there is a line between habit and addict but it's faint. Addiction is more complicated than the chemicals it becomes attached to. Breaking the chemical addiction is only one link in 'the accursed chain.'[37]

I hope it's clear – this is my Good Genius talking. My Invalid is with Sara.

1834 was a significant year for Sara. STC died. She began writing again. Prompted by De Quincey's accusations of STC's plagiarism, she began studying in order to defend her father. She wasn't free. Sara was pregnant seven times in ten years. Katie Waldegrave writes, 'Though she probably did not see it this way at the time, the poem ['Poppies'] was her first public defence of her father.'[38] Are Sara's pubic defences of her father, defences of her father? Or, by defending her father, was she able to defend herself?

To a Little Weanling Babe, who returned a kiss with great eagerness

Pretty Babe, 'tis all in vain,
Thou may'st suck and suck again,
But the lip, though soft it be,
Is no fount of milk for thee.
Baby, no! 'tis soft as silk,
But yet has nought to do with milk;
From the banks, where roses grow,
Lily streams shall never flow.

Baby when at man's estate,
Thou, with youthful hopes elate,
Seekest all things else above
Lady's fluent words of love;
Ne'er may lip, whence oft in dreams,
Flow for thee those nectar streams,
Dry as bloomless desert prove
When thou askest love for love. [39]

On breastfeeding

Breastfeeding doesn't turn me on but my nipples have always been part of sex. I find sex frustrating when I'm producing milk because this part of my body – a part that has always been linked to orgasms – is now assigned a different role. My nipples are cut off. My body is confused. I am a magician's assistant in a black box – cut in half. I can't enjoy sex until I give up breastfeeding and the magician waves a wand – to give me back my body. Motherhood owns the body so completely – it blocks all other feeling. This annihilation frightens me.

After four months, I try to give up breastfeeding Ted. I'm forced out of the house when my husband gives him that first bottle. He won't take it from me. He keeps rooting against my breast – mouth twisting and gumming the air. I go upstairs and listen to him wail through the bedroom floor. My body responds and my nipples buzz. The milk starts to come – they call this 'let down.' Apt. My top is soaked. I leave the house and sit in the car, weeping. I'm told that Ted cried himself to sleep.

In the middle of the night, when he cries for a night feed, my nipples drench the bed. I'm wearing breast pads but the milk pours – the mattress is soaked. Ted can smell my sweet yoghurty fug. My body radiates it. He can't understand why I won't give him my nipples. He throws his head backwards and forwards. Headbutts my chest. I waver. My breasts throb. Veins of milk bulge under the skin. The midwife said it was up to me. The NHS are militantly pro-breast – the benefits of breastfeeding *probably* outweigh the risks from the medication that passes through my milk. After that first night, I decide on a mid-course. The next evening, I give Ted a long bedtime feed. I take my pills. I sleep. I pump and dump the contaminated milk when I wake up. We replace it with formula. I repeat this process when Sid is born. I don't like the thought of someone else feeding them. Not even their dad. I am selfish. I am territorial. The midwives try to reassure me.

Sara weaned Edith early. At two months. She was convinced her milk was no good for Edith.

> My nervous debility and other unpleasant symptoms increased so much that I was obliged to think seriously of feeding my darling E. She now takes milk and oats with a little sugar in it out of the bottle. She was frightened by the spoon and at first there was some repugnance of the bottle – but she now takes it very well in general.[40]

Sara worried about how she would balance motherhood and intellectual life before she got married. She wrote, 'no one should quarrel with a woman devoting her leisure to literary pursuits instead of using it in making knick knacks or at the piano or with the pencil'[41] and 'if less worthy amusements were given up I believe almost every woman might devote some time to books.'[42] When Sara's mother moved in with her after Herbert's birth, she wrote:

> You cannot imagine how odd the change in Sara's habits appear to me – so different to those of her maiden days. Reading, writing, walking, teaching, dressing, mountaineering, and I may add, for the latter 10 years of that state – weeping – were her daily occupations with occasional visiting – Now, house orders, suckling, dress and undress – walking, sewing – morning visits and receiving – with very little study of Greek, Latin and English (no weeping!) make up ... her busy day.[43]

Sara resumed weeping in 1832. Sara's weeping allowed her time to study. Sara wrote most of *Phantasmion* during a prolonged stay in Ilchester – she aborted her journey home (from the in-laws in Ottery St Mary) – sent the children back with the nurse and refused to move. By giving up breastfeeding – and taking up weeping – she was allowed time away from the children. In this poem she insists that her lips have 'nought to do with milk.' Words cannot nourish a baby. She separates the intellectual from the mother. Hilary Marland raises the question of 'how far it is possible for Sara to have "learned" her illness' and suggests that her illness 'may have provided the framework for her escape from maternal duties to resume her writing.'[44] This makes it sound calculated, as though she was feigning illness. I'm repeatedly told that anxiety is part of the body's 'fight, flight or freeze' response to stress. The body wants to find safety. Books make me feel safe too.

When my nervousness comes on, I look for books. I chain-read. I light a new book with the smouldering nub of the last. I've always read compulsively but when I feel panic, I absorb myself in book after book. Reading is my only relief. People suggest watching a film or listening to music but reading works – those other activities are passive. I need something active. I can't let my mind walk away. I wonder how much my response is learned. How much my response to stress is, these days, a way of escaping motherhood?

In the second stanza this poem performs a volta. The poem addresses a boy. Sara had no trouble breastfeeding her son, Herbert – but the tangled relationship with literature and breast milk is cast onto advice for a young man. In 1843 Henry died, Sara became close friends – soon after – with the poet Aubrey De Vere. He was twelve years younger than Sara. Sara sent this poem to De Vere and entered it into her red manuscript book under 'Poems for De Vere.' In this context the first stanza takes on another dimension: it becomes more playful – mocking, even: 'Stop rooting against my lips, baby. There's no milk. All I have is words.'

According to Klein's object relations theory the breast is the first object of desire. The child needs to understand that the breast is attached to a person and doesn't exist for his pleasure, alone. However, all future pleasure will be measured against that first breast. 'These lips have nought to do with milk, De Vere. You won't find your mother's breast in my mouth.' Sara's not interested in lactophilia or becoming a mother figure. Breastfeeding doesn't turn her on. Sara's advice to the young man – both Herbert and De Vere: 'Don't forget – *everything* that comes from a woman's mouth is hollow. Only milk can be trusted – but, *come damn it* – my milk is gone!' This woman is losing her son. This woman is aging.

I think about mothers and sons a lot. Perhaps that's why I am drawn to this poem. I have two sons. I won't have any more children (I sprung a coil into my uterus as soon as Sid was born). My sister tells me that mothers with sons (and no daughters) are deranged – unbalanced. We over-attach. Sara had a daughter – was therefore, more rational than me. I, with my two sons, will turn into my mother-in-law. No-one will be good enough for my boys. I don't want to be the mad mother who clings to her babies – scared that another woman will displace me from the centre of their lives. I suspect that I already am that mother – glimpsed in the second stanza of this poem.

Sara's 'bloomless desart' contrasts with the 'banks where roses grow.' The mouth of the woman is barren when the boy gives love and expects love in return. I'm reminded that a woman has two mouths. Two sets of lips. Her words cannot nourish. Her vagina cannot either. Sara is emphasising sterility. Let's read the poem again, looking at that other set of lips speaking to a young lover from beneath her skirt. From inside her pants – 'Thou may'st suck and suck again,/ But the lip, though soft it be,/ Is no fount of milk for thee.' No young beau can extract cyprine – quintessence – from Sara's vagina. Maybe this mucky reading takes the poem a step too far, but Sara wasn't a buttoned up Victorian daughter. She was the daughter of STC.

> There are some of my Father's Poems which, though racy and energetic, are not *drawing roomy*. I would not call them, or any part of them, *coarse*, for this is to stigmatize them, which I would not do; for I consider them within the allowable range of a *man's* pen, and can hardly think it is to be decided that nothing is to be written and printed which it could not be good manners to read aloud in mixed company. The exceeding fastidiousness of the present age, one part of it at least, is more a sign of effeminacy and *luxurious* delicacy than of purity, as it seems to me.[45]

To Sara, STC's 'racy' language is not coarse, or *locker roomy* (to translate her into twenty-first century speak) – she was irritated by the censorship of her era. She considers all STC's poems 'within the allowable range of a *man's* pen.' For me, a poem that welds the grief of abandoning breastfeeding to the anxiety of losing a son and the fantasy of sex with a younger man, is within the 'allowable range of a *woman's* pen' – even a *Victorian* woman's pen.

From *Dreams*

II Time's Acquittal

1

I dreamed that, walking forth one summer's day
I chanced to meet old Time upon my way,
  And, full of spleen,
Taxed him with the mischief he had done
To me and thousands more beneath the sun
  Plain to be seen.

2

'Blush, blush for shame,' said I, 'to view this face
Despoiled by thee! – Canst thou one line retrace
  That erst was there?
I vow, ev'n I myself can scarce recall
It's heav'nly charm! – But I'm assured by all
  Old friends that it was fair.

3

'Come, thou canst bring it forth again, I know,
In pristine bloom – once more, ere yet I go
  Beneath the sod,
Present me to myself in finest feather
Of youth and health, – as when the mountain heather
  I lightly trod.'

4

Time seemed not all unwilling to comply:
Bade me look forth, and I should soon enjoy
   An apparition.
I looked: like morn slow-kindling in the skies
A dawn of rosy cheeks and sunny eyes
   Enriched my vision.

5

Cried I, 'This is the strangest thing on earth.
Two faces here I see – both full of mirth,
   And one much bolder
And broader too, like peony dispreads,
Than mine, when wreathed in curls and garlanded
   I look no longer old.'

6

My children's faces! Time, I did thee wrong
Thou'st made me doubly blooming glad and strong! –
   Let my light wane –
Since stars new-ris'n my downward path are cheering
And for one radiance, now fast disappearing,
   Thou giv'st me twain.[46]

On a mother's body

Sid is five. We are in my bedroom – I am getting dressed. He is bouncing on the bed. He stops. His hair is browned at the ends with sweat. His cheeks are pinked. His vividness always surprises me. From such a formless conception –

this boy! Like a cartoon – all bright colours – his crisp edge punched through the air.

'Mummy, I don't want to get fat when I grow up,' he says.

'I don't think you will,' I say.

He looks at me. I am naked.

'But you are,' he says.

He is five, but he deliberated over those words. I want to slap him. This son is capable of cruelty. I am tempted to say, 'Yes, I am fat now, but look at pictures of me before I had you. I wasn't fat. Why do you think I am fat?' I don't say that – it could be emotional abuse. Sometimes I think abuse should go both ways in this mother-child couple. Sometimes I think I'm in an abusive relationship with my son. Sid's tantrums are extreme. Ugly. Unpredictable. In a café he smashed a plate and bit my arm because I ordered the wrong cake. A ring of teeth marks opened – like blue-black petals. Contrast: he is unreservedly – totally, affectionate. He still likes to fall asleep in my arms. I like to fall asleep in his.

My body is different to my before-children-body. The antidepressants cause weight gain. My stomach is silvered in slug trails of stretch marks. Naked, my flesh looks melted, like wax. When I gave birth to them – they birthed this new body. I acquit them of blame – they didn't choose to be born but I am too petty to acquit Sid's cruelty.

Sara was beautiful. She was a renowned beauty. She was little and delicate. She had dark hair and big eyes. She knew she was beautiful but was dismissive of beauty. In 1826 she wrote, 'On the Disadvantages Resulting from the Possession of Beauty,'[47] in this essay she acknowledges the transience of physical beauty. She understands – at twenty-four! – that aging strips women of their looks. She concludes that it is understandable to be drawn to beauty but ultimately, it is deceptive. Nope, Sara says, truth isn't beauty. Beauty isn't truth![48] Beauty tricks us into 'fastening our attention too exclusively on what is external.'[49] Even the beauty found in nature – a flower or a landscape – distracts us from looking at the soul. This makes her sound stuffy. She wasn't – not always.

The image of the children, 'like morn slow-kindling in the skies/ A dawn of rosy cheeks and sunny eyes' is dosed with sugar. The sweetness constricts my throat. My mouth floods with saliva (the face-mouth's cyprine) – preparing to vomit (rather than orgasm). The peony opens – 'dispreads.' Abundance. Thick, wet petals. I like peonies but there is something profuse about their petalling froth. Gasping. The mother's body is weakened by this peony, it saps all energy.

The peonies in my garden are always covered in small, pale aphids – and ants. I've watched the ants. I've read about them. Ants farm aphids. The behaviour of the ants is much more sinister than the parasitic aphids. The children in this poem make me think of those ants running up and down the stems of the peonies – 'milking' excrement from the aphids – drinking the sugary juice until the aphid bodies shrivel and die. In my mind, I can't pull peonies away from those aphids – and ants.

Sara logged every change in her vaginal discharge. On 31st of October 1836, when she was recovering from a bout of nervousness, away from Henry and the home, she wrote, 'I have a good deal of whites at this time. This looks as if there was irritation of the uterus, which is a cause or sign of nervous weakness.'[50] The 'whites' (or leukorrhea) are also a sign of pregnancy. On the 14th of November she wrote, 'Alas

Alas! Took an anodyne last night at 9 o'clock combined with something to promote my menses. Just knowing I had done so I was terrified and perplexed. I had a most miserable night.' Why was she terrified and perplexed? Because she took 'something' along with her opium? Was the emmenagogue (used to – *ahem* – 'regulate her periods') wormwood? Parsley apiole? Not all emmenagogues cause abortion. Most do.

Sara returned home – almost recovered – when she'd distilled blood from her vagina. Sara was scared of children – of having more children. The children in the poem are scary. They bloom. They cloy. Their dawn light shrivels everything beneath. The emmenagogue might have been used to regulate her periods but 'terrified and perplexed' makes more sense if Sara was using an abortifacient when she suspected she was pregnant. I doubt she would be able to admit it to herself – she was a pious Christian, but her obsession with regeneration, years later, might have been a way of purging subconscious guilt.[51]

The mother is obliterated at the end of this poem. Time is acquitted but the children are not. The children rise and the mother withers. On first reading the poem sounds like Victorian sentiment but the tone reminds me of her father's confession, familiar to all parents but fleeting – unspoken (and unpublished by STC):

> Those little Angel Children (woe is me!)
> There have been hours when, feeling how they bind
> And pluck out the Wing-feathers of my Mind,
> Turning every Error to Necessity,
> I have half-wish'd they never had been born!
> That seldom! But sad Thought …

For my Father on his lines called 'Work Without Hope'

Father, no amaranths e'er shall wreathe my brow, –
Enough that round thy grave they flourish now: –
But Love 'mid my young locks his roses braided,
And what cared I for flow'rs of a deeper bloom?
Those too seemed deathless – here they never faded,
But, drenched and shattered, dropped into the tomb.

Ne'er was it mine t'unlock rich founts of song,
As thine it was, ere Time had done thee wrong: –
But ah! How blest I wandered nigh the stream,
Whilst Love, fond guardian, hovered o'er me still!
His downy pinions shed the tender gleam
That shone from river wide or scantiest rill.

Now, whether Winter 'slumbering, dreams of Spring',
Or, heard far off, his resonant footsteps fling
O'er Autumn's sunburnt cheek a paler hue,
While droops her heavy garland here and there,
Nought can for me those golden gleams renew,
The roses of my shattered wreath repair,
Yet Hope still lives, and oft, to objects fair
In prospect pointing, bids me still pursue
My humble tasks: – I list – but backwards turn
Objects for ever lost still struggling to discern.[52]

On work and hope

Sara often quoted this poem:

> All Nature seems at work. Slugs leave their lair—
> The bees are stirring—birds are on the wing—
> And Winter slumbering in the open air,
> Wears on his smiling face a dream of Spring!
> And I the while, the sole unbusy thing,
> Nor honey make, nor pair, nor build, nor sing.
>
> Yet well I ken the banks where amaranths blow,[53]
> Have traced the fount whence streams of nectar flow.
> Bloom, O ye amaranths! bloom for whom ye may,
> For me ye bloom not! Glide, rich streams, away!
> With lips unbrightened, wreathless brow, I stroll:
> And would you learn the spells that drowse my soul?
> Work without Hope draws nectar in a sieve,
> And Hope without an object cannot live.[54]

Virginia Woolf ends her essay on Sara Coleridge:

> But she died at forty-eight,[55] leaving, like her father, a blank
>   page covered with dots, and two lines:
> Father, no amaranths e'er shall wreathe my brow —
> Enough that round thy grave they flourish now.[56]

Sara's poem doesn't end there. Sara didn't end there. Sara left more than two lines.

> 'Enough that round thy grave they flourish now: –'

Before the colon Sara establishes her achievements.

Work: She made the amaranths bloom for her father by securing his place as poet and philosopher. When STC died he was a minor poet, a squandered talent, a sot – by 1834 there were whispers of plagiarism. Sara became *the* authority on German metaphysics – by 1844 Elizabeth Barrett-Browning wrote that Sara, possessed 'perhaps more learning in the strict sense, than any female writer of the day.'[57] Sara was a busy person – always working. In 1847 Sara republished STC's *Biographia Literaria* – properly referencing Shelling. She wrote candidly about her father's addiction, framed it as an illness. She admitted STC's plagiarism, framed it as part of his genius (an idea she elaborated from De Quincey). She published several editions of STC's books (slipping her own essays underneath). She worked on STC's collected poems until her death – published shortly after she died. She called it putting the 'house in order.' It was more like building a house. 'Esteesee' was a brand and Sara was good at marketing. She worked for the family firm. She packaged STC for a Victorian audience – she kept his books in print. Without Sara, would he be one of the 'big six' Romantics?

Colon: pause. And a dash – she goes on. The poem stops talking about her father after the first colon. This poem isn't for her father; it isn't about his poem. This poem is about Sara (slipped underneath two lines on her dad). Only if you stop reading at the colon can you believe she sacrificed her amaranths to tend to his. The poem continues: – Sara didn't wreathe her own brow in amaranths because she chose roses – and Henry (who braided roses into her hair). This poem is dated shortly after Henry died. She insists the roses never faded. They drop and shatter – bursting and fragmenting. The sodden petals fall apart without withering. Let's cut her some slack – she was newly widowed – she's allowed a few fibs. There's more truth in the ambivalence of 'downy pinions' – soft and protective – and a trap. Wing-clipped. When Henry died, Sara was free of childbearing! She became sole editor of STC. Sara didn't think she sacrificed her intellectual life for her father. She sacrificed it by becoming a wife and mother. At the end of this poem she is unable to see what she might have done if she hadn't chosen marriage and children – but she chooses to go forward.

Hope: Sara wrote this poem in 1843. She went on to write many more essays, poems and letters. She had more projects planned when she died in 1852 – aged forty-nine. This poem wasn't the end.

Sara once said she felt closest to her dad when reading his marginalia. Sara had the best qualifications to read her father – *punctum*, love and empathy. I have similar qualifications to read Sara. Ted is nearly ten. There are times when I feel like I've lost ten years of my life. Times 'when, feeling how they bind/ And pluck out the Wing-feathers of my Mind' — I'm not going to finish that thought. It's not fair or true. This is only one part of my story. Our story. The paths I didn't choose for ten years are overgrown, but I doubt there are any mythical amaranths in the undergrowth. It's healthier to think of those ten years as one of Sara's colons: pause and —

Blister packs

[*A translation of Poppies*]

If my son looked in my drawer
he would see rows of bubbles,
seeds in their shucks,
beans cuddled
in pockets of air. Some opened,
the husks bare
where the peeled foil
pops its silver.
The discarded skins: petals
scattered beneath makeup.
To him this would be snap, crackle, pop.

His face would remain dusty-smooth
like my tiny moons.
No line through his brow;
my face is the scored side:
a line to break – to wean.

They pattered my throat
just as he uncurled in the light.
The packets would rattle in his fat fist
without any grasp
that mummy needs these seeds
to pull morning –
like a bright magician's scarf
from the night.

Quickening

'there is no such thing as reproduction only acts of production'

Maggie Nelson, *The Argonauts*

On New Year's Day we climb Thorpe Cloud.
You say you can feel your heart beep
in your hands— pulsing in your gloves.

I remember dread that first formed—
cast from thread of piss on a stick.

After twelve tense weeks— with a wand
they divined your heartbeat from my
belly—not a beep— a deep thump.

I watched in case their faces betrayed
things I didn't want said and dreamed
your shape from clouds on a black screen.

At this point: where sky, moor, mountain, meet
and merge in January light. You are pitched—
grasping your beeping vein in your hands.

Notes

1/ Sara Coleridge, *Collected Poems*, edited by Peter Swaab, (Manchester: Carcanet, 2007), p186.
2/ Letter to Edward Quillinan, 31 March 1849, quoted in Peter Swaab, *Regions of Sara Coleridge's Thought: Selected Literary Criticism*, (New York: Palgrave MacMillan, 2012), p185.
3/ S T Coleridge, *Biographia Literaria*, ed. Sara Coleridge, (London: Pickering, 1847), pcxliv.
4/ Roland Barthes, *Camera Lucida*, (London: Vintage, 1993), p27.
5/ Virginia Woolf, *Death of a Moth and other essays*, (London: Penguin, 1960), p73.
6/ Journal, 3 November 1848, quoted in Swaab, *Regions*, p23.
7/ "quintessence, n.". OED Online. Oxford University Press.
8/ "laudanum, n.". OED Online. Oxford University Press.
9/ Lisa Robertson, 'In conversation with Madison Bycroft,' *Gong Farmer, Shit Stirrer and the Maiden of Grief*. 1646, 25 January 2019.
10/ Jeffery Barbeau, *Sara Coleridge: Her life and Thought*, (New York: Palgrave MacMillan, 2014), p130.
11/ Journal, 28 October 1848, quoted in Swaab, *Regions*, p41.
12/ Letter to Derwent Coleridge. Ibid., p43.
13/ Letter to Mary Pridham Coleridge, 14 August 1851, Ibid., p200.
14/ Swaab, *Regions*, pxxi.
15/ Sara Coleridge, *Collected Poems*, pp62-63.
16/ 29 August 1832, 'Diary of her children's early years,' Harry Ransom Centre, Texas.
17/ Quoted in Katie Waldegrave, *The Poets' Daughters*, (London: Hutchinson, 2013), p143.
18/ Letter to Derwent Coleridge, 6 June 1825, quoted in Swaab, *Regions*, pxii.
19/ Letter to Isabella Fenwick, 7 July 1847. Ibid., p40.
20/ Sandra M. Gilbert and Susan Gubar, *The Madwoman in the Attic: The Woman Writer and the Nineteenth-Century Literary Imagination*, Second Edition, (New York: Yale University Press, 2000), p49.
21/ Quoted in Swaab, *Regions*, pxiv.

22/ Sara Coleridge, *Collected Poems*, pp70-71.
23/ Sara wrote an essay: 'Nervousness,' in 1834, (Bradford Mudge, *Sara Coleridge A Victorian Daughter: Her Life and Essays.* New York: Yale University Press, 1989). The essay – set out as a dialogue between an 'Invalid' and 'Good Genius' explores the symptoms of her illness. Sara writes 'we must take instructions from our own *best* selves – which abstract conception I here personify by the name Good Genius & into the mouth of this Good Genius I shall put the results of my own long deliberations on the subject of those disorders which affect the mind.' Waldgrave calls this essay an early invention of talking therapy. It does read like a Cognitive Behavioural Therapy exercise. However, Sara was a fan of Landor's *Imaginary Conversations* and was probably playing with this form.
24/ 'Fireside Anacreontic,' quoted in Dennis Low, *The Literary Protégées of the Lake Poets,* (Aldershot: Ashgate, 2006), p130.
25/ Letter to Henry Nelson Coleridge, 24 September 1832, quoted in Mudge, p57.
26/ 'Diary of her children's early years,' HRC.
27/ Dora Wordsworth's presentation copy of *Pretty Lessons in Verse for Good Children,* quoted in Swaab, *Regions,* p4.
28/ To Emily Trevenen, 7 January 1835. Ibid., p6.
29/ To Mary Pridham July 1834. Ibid., p5.
30/ 'Diary of her children's early years,' July 1840, HRC.
31/ William Wordsworth, 'Ode: Imitations of Immortality from Recollections of Early Childhood,' line 114.
32/ Feldman eds, *British Women Poets of the Romantic Era: An Anthology,* (London: The John Hopkins University Press, 1997), p520.
33/ Letter to Derwent Coleridge, 1825, quoted in Low, p128.
34/ 'Diary of her children's early years,' August 27 1832, HRC.
35/ Sara Coleridge, *Memoirs and Letters of Sara Coleridge,* edited by her daughter, fourth edition, (London: Henry S. King & Co., 1875), p10.
36/ 'Nervousness' quoted in Mudge, p209.
37/ De Quincey claims he, 'untwisted, almost to its final links, the accursed chain which fettered me,' (Thomas De Quincey, *Confessions of an English Opium-Eater and*

Other Writings, (London: Penguin, 2003), p4. De Quincey's claims were exaggerated.
38/ Waldegrave, *The Poets' Daughters*, p149.
39/ Sara Coleridge, *Collected Poems*, p168.
40/ 'Diary of her children's early years' 12 September 1832, HRC.
41/ Letter to Louisa Powles, 27 March 1829, quoted in Waldegrave, *The Poet's Daughters*, p128.
42/ Letter to Louisa Powles, 27 July 1829, Ibid., p129.
43/ Mrs STC to Emily Trevenen, 27 February 1832. Ibid., p140
44/ Hilary Marland, *Dangerous Motherhood: Insanity and Childbirth in Victorian Britain,* (Basingstoke: Palgrave, 2004), pp90-91.
45/ Letter to John Taylor Coleridge, June 1843, quoted in Swaab, *Regions,* p33.
46/ Sara Coleridge, *Collected Poems*, pp160-161.
47/ Mudge, pp187-200.
48/ Though Sara admired 'Keats excessively' she felt that to 'be always reading Shelley and Keats would be like living on quince-marmalade.' Letter to Hartley Coleridge, January 20th 1845, *Memoir*, p224.
49/ Mudge, p200.
50/ Diary of her children's early years, 31 October 1836, HRC.
51/ Sara spent the final few years of her life writing a long essay called 'Regeneration'. Jeffrey Barbeau suggests that, prompted by the death of all those unbaptised babies, she was unable to reconcile her faith with the Church's teaching on original sin.
52/ Sara Coleridge, *Collected Poems*, p156.
53/ '"amarant(h), n.". An imaginary flower reputed never to fade; a fadeless flower (as a poetic conception), OED Online. Oxford University Press.
54/ Samuel Taylor Coleridge, 'Work Without Hope,' *Selected Poetry and Prose,* (London: Penguin, 1957), p108.
55/ Sara was forty-nine when she died.
56/ Woolf, *Death of a Moth*, p77.
57/ Quoted in Low, p184.

Bibliography

Manuscripts

Coleridge, Sara. 'Diary of her Children's Early Years.' Harry Ransom Research Centre, University of Texas.

Books and articles

Barbeau, Jeffery. *Sara Coleridge: Her life and Thought*. New York: Palgrave MacMillan, 2014.

Barthes, Roland. *Camera Lucida*. London: Vintage, 1993.

Coleridge, Sara. *Collected Poems*. Edited by Peter Swaab. Manchester: Carcanet, 2007.

Coleridge, Sara. *Memoirs and Letters of Sara Coleridge*. Edited by Edith Coleridge. Fourth Edition. London: Henry S. King & Co., 1875.

Coleridge, Samuel Taylor. *Biographia Literaria*. Edited by Sara Coleridge. London: Pickering, 1847.

Coleridge, Samuel Taylor. *Selected Poetry and Prose*. Selected by Kathleen Raine. London: Penguin, 1957.

Cox, J. L., Holden, J. M., and Sagovsky, R. (1987). *Detection of postnatal depression: Development of the 10-item Edinburgh Postnatal Depression Scale*. British Journal of Psychiatry

De Quincey, Thomas. *Confessions of an English Opium-Eater and Other Writings*. London: Penguin, 2003.

De Quincey, Thomas. *Recollections of the Lakes and The Lake Poets*. London: Penguin, 1970.

Sandra M. Gilbert and Susan Gubar. *The Madwoman in the Attic: The Woman Writer and the Nineteenth-Century Literary Imagination*. Second Edition. New York: Yale University Press, 2000.

Feldman, Paula ed. *British Women Poets of the Romantic Era: An Anthology*. London: The John Hopkins University Press, 1997.

Griggs, Leslie. *Coleridge Fille*. London: Oxford University Press, 1940.

Heti, Sheila. *Motherhood*. London: Harvill Secker, 2018.

Marland, Hilary. *Dangerous Motherhood*. London: Palgrave MacMillan, 2004

Mudge, Bradford. *Sara Coleridge A Victorian Daughter: Her Life and Essays*. New York: Yale University Press, 1989.

Low, Dennis. *The Literary Protégées of the Lake Poets*. London: Routledge, 2016.

Peter Swaab ed. *Regions of Sara Coleridge's Thought: Selected Literary Criticism*. New York: Palgrave MacMillan, 2012.

Waldegrave, Katie. *The Poets' Daughters*. London: Hutchinson, 2013.

Woolf, Virginia. *Death of a Moth and Other Essays*. London: Hogarth, 1942.

Acknowledgments

Thanks to the staff at the Harry Ransom Centre at the University of Texas in Austin for access to Sara's archive.
Earlier versions of some of these essays were first published in *Empty Mirror*.
An earlier version of 'Quickening' was published in Stand.
I'm extremely grateful to Lila Matsumoto for reading each draft – I couldn't have written these essays without her.
Thank you to Christian for all of your support.
Finally, thank you to Sara for your honesty – I enjoyed our conversations.

LAY OUT YOUR UNREST

www.ingramcontent.com/pod-product-compliance
Lightning Source LLC
Chambersburg PA
CBHW061344040426
42444CB00011B/3080